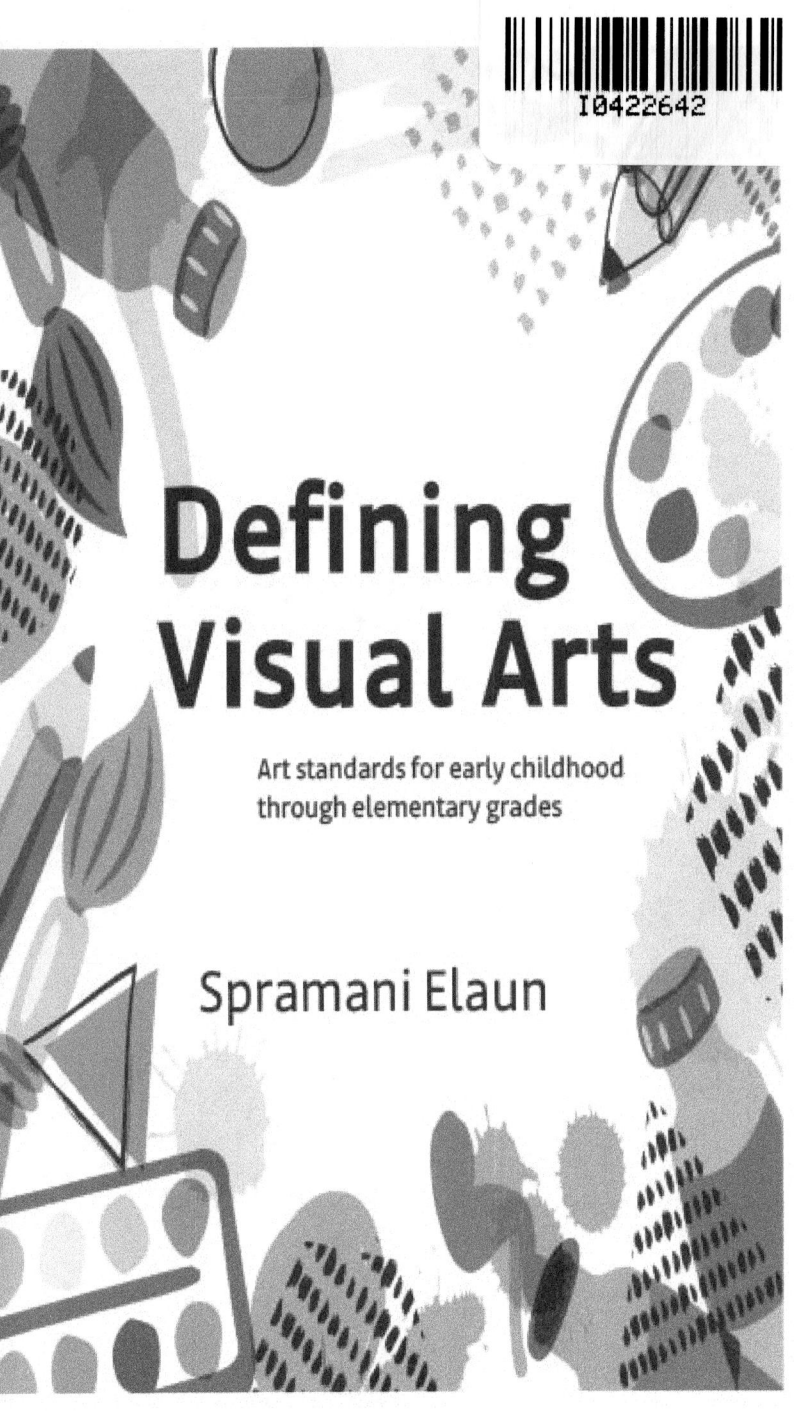

Defining
Visual Arts

Art standards for early childhood
through elementary grades

Spramani Elaun

Defining Visual Arts

Defining Visual Arts

Art standards for early childhood
through elementary grades

Second Edition

Spramani Elaun

Nature of Art® Publishing, California

Nature of Art® Publishing
P.O. Box 443 Solana Beach, California 92075

Second edition published
Printed in the United States of America
ISBN-978-0-9916264-5-8

All artwork and photographs were taken in an art
classroom or at special art events hosted
By Spramani Elaun.

Also By Spramani Elaun

The Way Children Make Art
Kids Painting
Early Childhood Art Guide
Nurturing Children in the Visual Arts Naturally
Clay Play
Kids Color Theory
Introducing Visual Arts to the Montessori Classroom
Montessori Art – Early Childhood Guide
Montessori Art – The Essential Elementary Guide

This book is dedicated to every
teacher on every continent.

Connect With Spramani Online:

EcoKidsArt.com
Montessori-Art.com
Nature-of-art-kids.com
Spramani.com

Facebook.com/nature.of.art
Instagram.com/nature.of.art.kids
Linkedin.com/in/ecokidsart

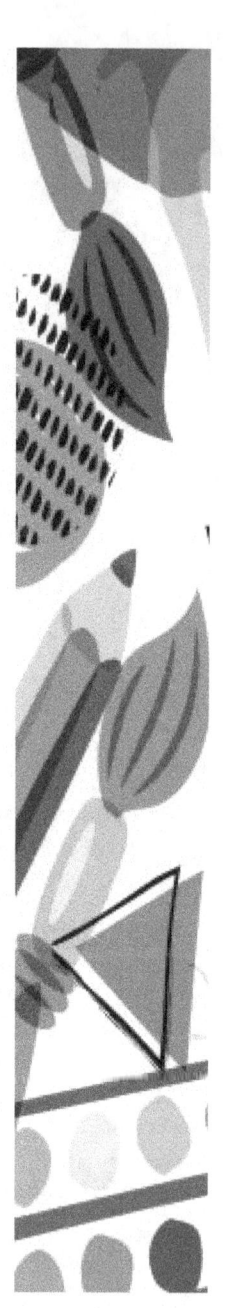

Contents

Chapters

Defining Visual Arts

INTRODUCTION

Focus of this Book

After studying visual arts as a professional artist, homeschooler, a children's art teacher, and now an international Montessori art teacher trainer, I saw the urgent need to clarify and define visual arts for the young student.

Across continents, I've witnessed how most educators need a clear description of what needs to be taught, a precise explanation of what should be included in the art curriculum and why. I have also noticed the blurred lines that occur when educational standards intrude on the very nature of an artist's ability to express creativity, an essential human trait. It is important to help nations pass down to their children and future generations the heritage of their cultural arts and design.

As I've traveled to different states and countries and taught to many different pedagogies, I've come to an understanding of what the visual arts look like for early childhood through adolescence across the board.

This book is designed as a quick guide to identify what constitutes visual arts, why children should learn visual arts, and what areas to teach. After you have read this book, you might want to read further on how children evolve cognitively into artists, learn about different art teaching methods for children, and dive deeper into technique and art lesson ideas. You can find more on these topics in my other visual arts book series.

Artworks explain who we are... what we've witnessed... and our perceptions of these ideas.

Spramani Elaun

Defining Visual Arts

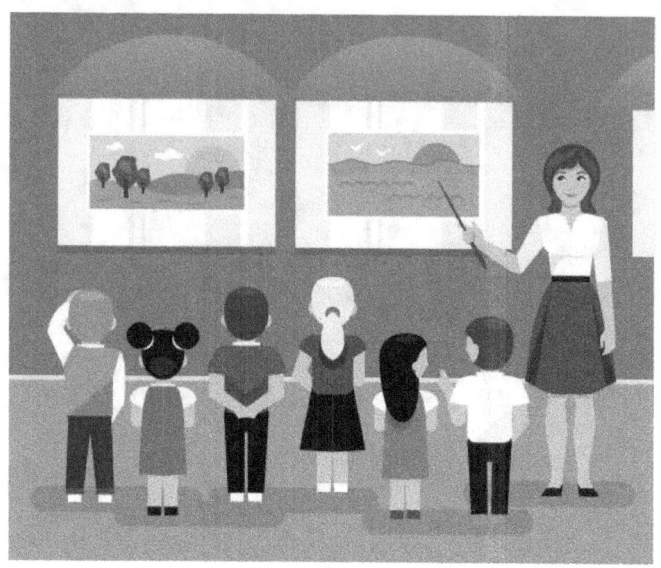

Chapter One

WHY VISUAL ARTS IS IMPORTANT TO TEACH

Why teach visual arts?

- The arts are a unique form of human communication
- It fosters critical-thinking and problem-solving skills
- Arts are tools for multicultural understanding
- The visual arts are a way to understand the social, historical, and cultural contexts of work from students' own countries
- It cultivates pleasure and enjoyment and fosters a sense of well-being
- The arts stimulate brain development during the art-making process
- It helps children enter creative flow states, which leads to innovative, creative thinking
- It regulates Stress

Defining Visual Arts

Chapter Two

WHAT ART LITERACY MEANS

What is art literacy?

Art literacy means providing students the opportunity to work through the artistic process, through their education, using visual arts standards. To give you a better background on how the arts standards came to exist and how they were formed, artists across the world were surveyed through college education boards to understand what the artistic process means.

Artists of all walks of life, both in visual arts and performing arts, were surveyed. This study revealed the processes that artists work through, from visionary conceptual ideation to a completed creation.

Educational researchers surveyed people like musicians and studied how they create music, how they write music, and how they perform. They met with sculptors and studied how a sculptor comes up with conceptual ideas and brings them to form.

They even studied how visual imaginative ideas come to life, how they end up in a museum, and how the ideas support reflection within oneself or the community. They studied painters from the Old Masters to modern-day artists, trying to understand what it is to be creative, how to come up with sketched ideas from imagination, and how to develop completed paintings.

Once these findings were evaluated, the data was put into a matrix of artistic stages. Then artistic standards were created to help guide educators. We now call this the Artistic Process.

The artistic process comprises four actions:

- *Investigate*
- *Imagine*
- *Construct*
- *Reflect*

Better Understanding the Artistic Process

Artistically literate means students must engage in real-time dynamic creative processing, using a variety of proper visual art mediums and materials relevant to visual arts.

Students should have opportunities during visual art lessons to practice using their imagination, investigate through exploring, construct their own artworks, and collaborate with other students on group projects.

They should also be able to reflect by sharing ideas and concepts within their community.

Investigation – Students should have the opportunity to investigate different art projects and a variety of mediums and techniques through exploration, examination, and discovery.

Imagination – Students should have the opportunity to imagine an original mental image or concept. Children should brainstorm ideas, solve problems, organize conceptualized concepts, and plan or blueprint how to create their finalized conception.

Construction – Children should solve problems by constructing and arranging the elements and principles of design, using fine art materials and mediums and artistic techniques.

Reflection – Children should have opportunities to reflect on their art creations either verbally or in writing, describing their artworks or their process. Preparing artworks to display in a gallery setting is another way to reflect.

What are visual arts?

Visual arts can be two- or three-dimensional forms visible to the human eye. Visual arts are created objects made by a human. These forms are usually created to evoke emotions or ideas.

Visual arts may be intended for an audience or solely for the creator. Visual art forms can be created with many different types of materials, in many colors, or in simple black and white hues. Visual art creations can also take on different forms, shapes, or contours.

What is an artist?

An artist is a person skilled in the fine arts or design. An artist develops skills in various media, using a variety of tools and materials. An artist can also employ unique techniques of their own design.

An artist may be paid for their skills or sell their

creations. On the other hand, an artist may never share their created works. Either way, the artist develops his or her skills over time. An artist is also known as the creator of a visionary idea.

Who are visual arts standards for?

Educators.

Why do visual arts standards exist?

To help teachers understand what it means to be artistically literate and to help develop curriculum, provide an approach to instruction, and evaluate artistic progression. Visual arts standards for children had never been comparable from country to country, state to state, school to school, or even teacher to teacher, until these standards were put into place recently.

Are visual arts standards similar to Common Core?

No.

Visual arts standards help support artistic literacy. There are local, state, and national agencies currently working together to help unify arts standards nationwide. The National Coalition for Core Arts Standards (NCCAS) has made these efforts in the US and provides additional guidance online.

I provide links to these websites at the back of this book, in the resource section. In your own country, you might find this information through your local education system boards.

The NCCAS are for educators teaching pre-K through high school. The standards were established in 2014, by teachers, for teachers. The visual arts standards emerged from research into understanding the artistic process.

The arts standards are voluntary, not mandatory. Most standards are a model of structures to follow. The arts standards help teach children artistic literacy from school to school across the nation.

Check your local or state education department for any mandatory guides. Most state standards are similar to these national standards. The visual arts standards vary from grade to grade.

Understanding the arts standards

Here is what is very important for you to know and understand. The visual arts standards do not tell you what to teach your students, meaning they do not tell you which area to focus on, like drawing or painting, or whether or not to use a specific medium, like crayons or paints, or even what techniques to explore. The standards do not determine how learning in the arts will be delivered.

The standards create artistic literacy by giving teachers four basic artistic process actions that children should experience while creating artworks. Artistic literacy develops by doing four actions from project to project: investigate, imagine, construct, and reflect. If every art lesson you teach takes the student through the four actions, you are meeting the national visual arts standards.

In all my experience and research, no specific curriculum with a proper scope and sequence is offered. So if you focus on a specific pedagogy or value system, you have the freedom to create your own curriculum based on your own criteria. This book will further guide you on what areas to teach, your teaching focus in each discipline, why it's important to teach it, and what constitutes artistic development.

Defining Visual Arts

Chapter Three

THE AREAS OF VISUAL ARTS TO STUDY

I've identified the important skills needed to advance as an artist. These skills can be developed by focusing on five areas of art study. Elementary students should have a foundation in these areas. I call them the Five Domains. I feel these areas lay a good foundation for learning more advanced concepts needed in fine art or design. The Five Domains are what we should be teaching in a quality visual arts education.

The Five Domains:

> Drawing
> Painting
> Color theory (color mixing)
> Clay modeling (sculpture)
> Crafting and constructing

There are two other areas of visual arts to study, which are not included in my five domains:

Architecture
Multimedia arts

Architecture is the study of the design and structure of buildings. Multimedia is the study of fine arts created for digital screens using hardware and software.

I feel children should first focus on the Five Domains as a primer foundation, then in upper grades, transition into learning the other two domains. However, if there are not enough hours to spend on the extra two areas during the elementary years, I would not be too concerned about covering them. The middle- and high-school grades are better opportunities to grasp those concepts.

I've observed over the years that students who have not spent any time creating in the Five Domains first struggle in two-dimensional perspective drawing and three-dimensional spatial understanding, which is needed to have spatial understanding in both architecture and multimedia design.

Yes, sometimes children jump on multimedia platforms and create great artworks, but it is always good for a child to get a solid foundation in the Five Domains before studying the other two areas.

What you teach in the Five Domains

Drawing

Drawing is a two-dimensional art form that children commonly learn by using various drawing mediums on flat paper. These drawing lessons should begin by focusing on skill-building movements to create basic Art Elements. As students progress, they develop the ability to make controlled line marks and create geometric and organic shapes. Check out my sequential Drawing Curriculum– 49 lessons for more guidance.

Painting

Painting is a dynamic two-dimensional art form that involves the action of creating brushstrokes. Through brush marks, all elements and principles of design can be expressed.

Painting also encompasses printmaking, which utilizes different materials. Paintings can range from abstract marks to collaborative brushstrokes that form realistic imagery. Various surfaces such as canvas,

17

paper, cardboard, wood, and natural objects like rocks, leaves, or fabric can be used for painting. Additionally, painting can involve the use of unconventional objects besides paintbrushes.

Check out my sequential Painting Curriculum – 57 brushstroke Lessons and Painting Works –Art Album.

Color theory

Color theory is a crucial aspect of art that teaches artists how to manipulate color moods in their artworks. It not only provides valuable spatial learning opportunities but it also holds therapeutic benefits. The knowledge of color theory can be applied across various domains of art study.

To introduce color theory, I recommend starting with primary colors: red, yellow, and blue (RYB) and then progress to mixing secondary colors. Elementary students can learn to create a twelve-step, full-spectrum color wheel using primary colors. Once they have a solid understanding of secondary color mixing, you can move on to teaching them about value gradients, tints, shades, tones, and complementary colors.

Color theory utilizes the same mediums as paint, so you will be using many of the same materials and tools from the painting area. By integrating color theory into art lessons, students can develop a deeper understanding of how colors interact and convey emotions in their artwork. You can also read my Kids Color Theory book and sequential Kids Color Theory curriculum – 37 lessons for more guidance.

Clay modeling

Clay modeling is a three-dimensional art form that encompasses height, length, and width, allowing for the creation of solid geometric forms in space. It serves as a foundation for sculpture or ceramics. It occasionally utilizes sculpture tools.

Clay modeling offers numerous benefits, including the development of hand dexterity and sensorimotor skills. Through the tactile experience of working with clay, spatial information is wired in memory. Additionally, clay modeling aids in understanding three-dimensional space and form, which is one of the core Art Elements to teach.

For example, starting with basic forms like spheres, students can grasp the concept of solid geometric forms. As a primer, clay modeling lessons can focus on learning these fundamental forms before progressing to creating objects of interest such as fruit or animals.

Eventually, students can explore advanced sculpture techniques like carving, coil building, and clay relief work. There are various types of clay available, each with its own unique characteristics. You can find information on clay and tools in the art materials section of this book. You can also read my Clay Modeling curriculum – 29 lessons.

Crafting and constructing

Crafting and constructing typically result in three-dimensional artworks. The idea is to incorporate elements and mediums together by crafting or constructing by hand. This domain supports spatial, sensory, and tactile learning.

The Elements and Principles of Design can be applied to all craft projects. Some fundamental elements to grasp include colors, space, patterns, and textures. The principles aid in creating aesthetically pleasing crafts.

When children learn these basic principles, their handicrafts take on an artistic quality. They can arrange one or a combination of elements and decide which principles of art to incorporate into their final designs. This involves learning various skill sets, such as how to use artisan tools and work with raw materials.

For instance, consider crafting a leather keychain. You start by choosing the shape to cut out from raw leather, then designing intricate line patterns. Finally, you can embellish it by sewing colorful beads or adding paint to make it visually appealing. This domain also provides an opportunity to explore artisan techniques and crafts from different cultures or regions. You can even delve into the art and functional crafts of ancient civilizations, gaining insights into their fundamental needs and examining their craftsmanship.

Defining Visual Arts

Chapter Four

MEDIUMS AND MATERIALS

Now that you understand the five areas to teach, I want to go little bit deeper and tell you the different mediums, tools, and materials typically used in each area.

Drawing

Drawing is done with many different mediums: graphite pencil, crayon, color pencils, oil pastels, soft pastels, watercolor pencils, or charcoal.

You usually use smooth uncoated white paper as a surface. For charcoal and soft pastels, use charcoal paper only; any shade or color works well. Other tools are an eraser and a pencil sharpener.

Painting

Painting is usually done with paint mediums and paintbrushes, making brush strokes on many different types of surfaces. Mediums to paint with are acrylic, watercolor, tempera, finger paint, gouache, watercolor pencils, watercolor crayons, India ink, Chinese ink, or dry watercolor cakes.

Surfaces can include canvas, cardboard, wood, sticks, rocks, watercolor paper, recycled surfaces, or fabric. Other tools include paintbrushes in different brush sizes, palettes to hold and mix paint colors, napkins or rags for cleanup, and wash jars.

For printmaking monoprints, common printmaking tools include water-based ink, carving tools, stamp blocks to carve or stamp shapes, ink-mixing trays, and an ink brayer (a hand roller).

Color Theory

Color theory is done with different paint mediums. You will want to start with primary colors plus black and white. You will use basically all the same mediums and tools from the painting area. You will want to have a color wheel chart showing kids how primary colors mix into secondary colors.

Clay Modeling and Sculpting

Typical clays come in many forms of natural organic or inorganic matter. Clays harden either by air-drying overnight or by baking. Most clays that dry can be painted on.

Other types of modeling clay are non-hardening, and these stay malleable. Clays come in many colors; there are even bright color choices.

Here are great clays for children to form with: plasticine clay (will not harden); Magic Model (can air-dry overnight, then be painted on); natural beeswax (can harden at cooler temperatures, then be re-formed when the beeswax warms up again); polymer clay (can bake and harden into small sculptures); and plaster-type clays to pour into molds.

Crafting and constructing

Many different mediums can be used to craft or build with. You can incorporate sewing, gluing, cutting, paper folding, wood making, 3D structures, or weaving.

Design, pattern, texture, and structure are important. Using either hands or tools is subject to the artist's interest. Common materials might be: string, natural materials, paper, fabric, yarn, wood, cardboard, or just about any material can be crafted. Check out my sequential Crafting & Building Curriculum– lessons for more guidance.

Chapter Five

THE ART LANGUAGE WE TEACH

The Elements and Principles of Design

These special terms and their meanings are what we study in the visual arts. The Elements and Principles of Design are how we describe what we see in artworks. It is art's own language. It's virtually impossible to describe any artwork without using any elements and principles of design language.

In traditional fine arts school, The Elements and Principles of Design language helps give meaning to observation and technique. The list of elements and principles of design is long. There are many terms to study, such as texture, line, form, value, composition, etc.

By equipping students with this vocabulary, we teach them how to communicate what they see in their art, as well as how to describe their process and explain what they admire in artworks.

Elementary students are ready to learn art language. They are ready for fun, open-ended, and simple guided instruction on The Elements and Principles of Design. It takes years to learn how to observe and communicate in this language.

These terms are difficult to grasp and understand at first. Teaching The Elements and Principles of Design should start out very basic and then progress in the upper grades. Here are the elements and principles lower and elementary should learn first:

Line
Shape
Form
Color
Value

Space
Texture
Pattern
Two dimensions
Three dimensions
Concentric design
Symmetry
Composition

This list is appropriate for you to get started with early childhood and elementary students. As you are working with children in your art classroom, these are great terms to introduce.

You can point out the elements and principles when you are talking or describing artworks. Once you understand these terms, you can refer to them in the correct context while teaching visual arts. This will also help you build your confidence in art language. See the full definitions in the next chapter.

The Elements and Principles of Design vs. elements of art: I'd like to point out that I've noticed teachers using the term "elements of art," in kindergarten through primary grades, instead of using the full term, the "elements and principles of design."

It is a general list of the first seven elements. I just want to point this out because you may have come across the former term, which has the exact same meaning as the latter. It's just been shortened.

The Elements and Principles of Design – definitions Line

A line is created by a moving point in space. Lines can be two-dimensional and can create the illusion of three-dimensional space on a flat geometric plane. In artworks, lines can be descriptive, implied, or abstract. This element can be taught in all five domains. Lines can begin as straight or curved, vertical, horizontal, diagonal, zigzag, or broken.

Shape

Shape is two-dimensional and flat, limited to width and height. For instance, a flat shape like a square is derived from plane geometry, while a cube is a solid geometric form. Teaching shape is most effective in 2-D mediums such as painting, drawing, and crafting. Shapes can be classified as geometric or organic.

Color

Color consists of three properties: hue, value, and intensity. "Hue" is often used interchangeably with "color," like red, blue, or green. Colors can have high or low intensity, with high-intensity colors appearing bright and pure, while low-intensity colors are faint or dull.

The element of color can be taught in all five domains, with color theory lessons being the most effective introduction.

Form/Mass

Form is three-dimensional, possessing volume and having height, width, and depth. Solid geometric forms, such as a cube, sphere, or cylinder, exemplify this element. Form is best taught through clay modeling and crafts.

Value

Value is a fundamental element in art that refers to the lightness or darkness of a color. It can be described as a gradient of hues, ranging from light to dark. For example, a hue like red can have various values, such as light, medium, dark, or even darker shades of red.

Understanding value is crucial in drawing and painting as it helps create contrast and depth in artworks. Artists can utilize different values of color to create both light and dark marks, adding dimension and visual interest to their compositions.

Space

Space can be described in both two and three dimensions. In two dimensions, space is represented on a flat plane. Artists can arrange different Art Elements within this plane to create the illusion of depth and space.

In more advanced art, artists study linear perspective to create dimensional spaces in their drawings and paintings. By understanding the principles of linear perspective, they can effectively convey depth and create a sense of realism within their artwork.

When it comes to three-dimensional space, artists can manipulate the geographical placement or position of elements to create interesting spatial relationships and volumes. This allows for the creation of sculptures, installations, and other three-dimensional artworks that engage the viewer from multiple angles.

Texture

Texture can be described in two distinct ways. First, in a two-dimensional sense, artists can use marks and patterns to create the illusion of texture on a flat picture plane. By skillfully incorporating lines and shapes, they can make an image appear to have a certain tactile quality.

For instance, drawing scales using precise line marks on a fish can give the impression that it feels scaly. Second, artists can also create a tactile texture that can be physically felt sensorially. This type of texture engages our sense of touch rather than just our visual perception. An example of this would be stringing beads to create a beaded pattern; one can actually feel the texture by running their fingers across it.

Pattern

Pattern in art refers to the repetition of shapes, lines, colors, or other elements in a deliberate and organized manner. It is the arrangement of these repeated elements that creates a sense of rhythm and visual harmony within an artwork. Patterns can be simple or complex, and they can be found in various forms such as geometric designs, natural motifs, or abstract arrangements.

Artists often use patterns to add visual interest, create a sense of movement, or establish a decorative quality in their work. Overall, patterns play a crucial role in enhancing the visual appeal and coherence of an artwork.

3D

Three-dimensional shapes or artwork have height, width, and depth. This means they can be measured in three directions, making them look more realistic and solid. A great way to learn about 3D is through clay modeling and crafting, where you can create objects that you can actually touch and feel and that have mass.

2D

Two-dimensional forms or artwork have only height and width. They exist on a flat plane surface, like a piece of paper or a canvas. To understand 2D, you can study drawing, painting, and color theory. These domains help create pictures and designs that look flat but still have depth and visual interest.

Composition

Composition refers to how the visual elements or different parts are arranged in an artwork. It's like deciding where everything should go to make the artwork look its best. Artists plan out the composition before creating their art. It's like making a blueprint or a plan for how the elements and empty spaces will be arranged.

Concentric

Concentric designs have a common center or axis, but each pattern or shape has a different distance from the center. For instance, imagine a mandala with six concentric circle rings.

The design begins with a small circle in the middle center, and as you move out, larger circles expand outwards, all sharing the same center axis. However, the radius of each circle changes as you move away from the center. This means that the circumference and diameter of each circle become larger.

Symmetry

Symmetry is the quality of being made up of exactly similar parts that face each other or align around an axis. Symmetry can be divided into two equal and identical shapes. For example, if you were to cut a butterfly sample in half, the two sides would be mirror images of each other, showing mirror symmetry.

Defining Visual Arts

Chapter Six

HOW WE USE ART LANGUAGE TO DESCRIBE WHAT WE SEE IN ARTWORKS

In this area, I want to give you an example of how we use this language. I now want to describe how this all comes together and how you can actually speak and communicate about artworks to a student. Here is a picture of a painting I will describe using art language. I feel this will give you a good understanding of how The Elements and Principles of Design are used to communicate what we see in artworks.

I'm looking at this painting (fig 1.) called "Starry Night," an oil on canvas by Dutch post-impressionist painter Vincent Van Gogh.

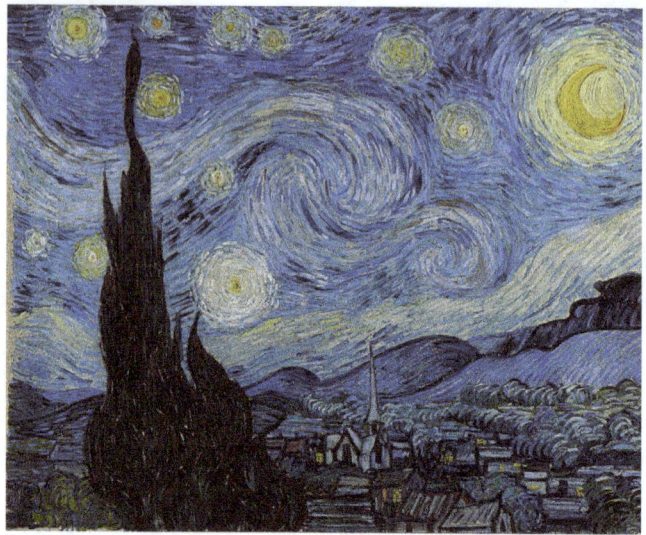

(fig 1.) called "Starry Night," an oil on canvas by Dutch post-impressionist painter Vincent Van Gogh.

I can see deep rich values of color created with oil paint. The artist used brushstrokes that look to me like thick, short brush lines. The brushstrokes go in many directions.

The thick brushstroke lines give the impression of a wood carving texture. I see Van Gogh's brilliant color choices; the different values of dark and light blue create a striking night study. In the far corner of the top right space, I see the moon.

I see the outline of the yellow moon's shape; it's a rounded crescent shape. I see thick, curved brushstrokes of yellow values tinted by white encircling this crest shape.

I feel as if there's movement of the clouds in the sky, created by the artist's choice of textured wavy marks. These small, short brushstrokes give a nice texture to the whole painting. Then I see the trees in the foreground of the painting.

It's almost like the trees are really close to me in the foreground, and the sky is far in the background. This gives us a three-dimensional perspective of the full landscape and horizon because of the shading of dark colors.

Then I want to point out the horizon line, which separates the sky from the earth. The horizon line from the sky to the mountaintops is contrasted by this thick brushstroke, giving us the illusion of distance, the middle ground of the painting.

And then I can see all the homes at the lower right space of the painting. The artist used the reflection of the moon and started with small lines and dashes of brilliant yellow and white to illuminate and contrast.

I can see all the reflections and the textures of the brushstrokes against the dark shades of paint. And I love the composition, how it looks like it's moving. It's a painting with motion.

I just described to you what The Elements and Principles of Design mean and how artists use the language in fine arts school to describe their artworks.

OK.

Do I think you should focus whole lessons around using this language?

Probably not at first. As art facilitators, our goal should be to introduce each one as children learn to incorporate these elements into their art.

You should definitely incorporate them into your art discussions to gradually build up this artistic language. While my description was at a high school level, it's important to take it slowly and use these concepts regularly to describe what you are pointing out.

You want to introduce the terminology, but I don't think you should focus your whole lesson on these terms by drilling kids and asking the students to speak only using this language or correct them when they don't.

It's something you have to ease into very gently. Just understanding that the terms exist and knowing how they are used in the context of art-making is a good start! You're most likely using them all the time in your conversations without realizing their relevance to visual arts education.

Introducing art terms to lower elementary students and guiding them to identify and incorporate these elements in their artworks is a valuable step in their artistic development. When discussing their work, encourage them to utilize the Art Elements you have introduced, enhancing their ability to articulate their creative choices.

For upper elementary students, it is time to take their skills to the next level by utilizing these elements in their designs. Encourage them to engage in critical thinking and problem-solving, applying principles such as composition balance, concentric design, and symmetry to their artwork. By incorporating these principles, they can create visually appealing and harmonious images.

It's important to emphasize that art language equips artists with the terminology needed to describe the choices they make in creating their imagery or constructed crafts. By using this language, students can effectively communicate their artistic decisions and intentions to others, fostering a deeper understanding of their own creative process.

Defining Visual Arts

TEACHING AN ARTIST'S TECHNIQUE

Artist's technique

I would now like to explain what an artist's technique is and how important it is to include in your teaching. An artist's technique means a way of doing something, or a special way an artist performs basic movements unique to their own style.

There are literally thousands of techniques you can teach children. The sky's the limit! You could teach them classical techniques from the masters like Van Gogh, Picasso, or even local modern-day artists you might know or those in museums close to your town.

Eric Carle

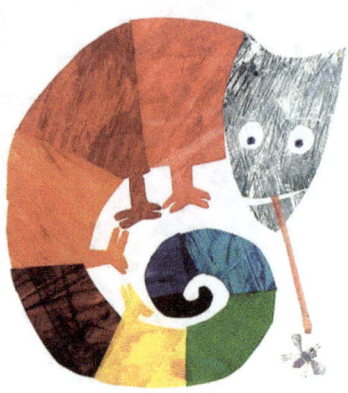

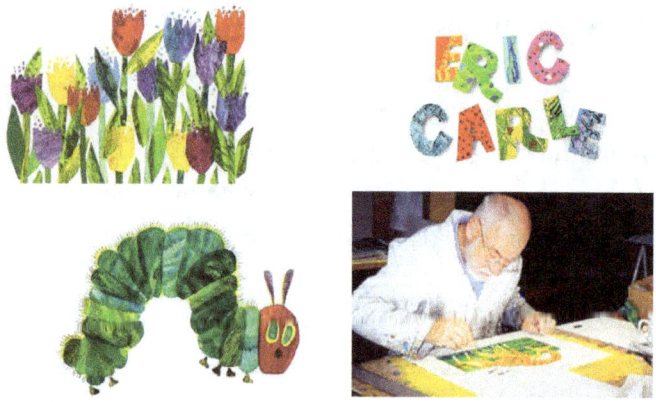

Eric Carle, a renowned American author and children's book illustrator. Figure 2.

The fundamental principle is to choose an artist who has created exemplary works that showcase the specific technique you intend to teach your students.

To provide you with an example of an artist's technique, let's consider Eric Carle, a renowned American author and children's book illustrator (figure 2.).

Carle's artworks possess a unique and instantly recognizable style. His technique involves beginning with watercolor-textured papers, hand-cutting the painted papers into various shapes, and ultimately layering these vibrant and cheerful images together.

By showcasing an artist in this manner, you can demonstrate to children a particular technique, including the step-by-step process the artist employed. This approach helps children grasp the concept of going through their own artistic process, which may involve creating textured watercolor papers, allowing them to dry, cutting them into layers, and crafting collages based on their own ideas. It's a valuable way to introduce kids to an artist's technique.

Here's another crucial reason why I recommend introducing an artist's technique from time to time: Imagine a table with paper and a bowl of crayons. To the casual observer, using crayons and paper is enjoyable, and there are plenty of creative possibilities with crayons.

However, I find it much more exciting when you can guide the children and say, "Now, I want to introduce you to a special technique that artists use with crayons and paper, known as 'wax resist.'"

You can then show them art samples and explain, "These were created by artists who use a wax resist technique with crayons." Suddenly, the children become inspired to experiment and create with guided direction.

I've experienced this myself year after year in my art studio. Children would eagerly enter my studio, full of excitement, but sometimes they lacked the confidence to start creating. They might not have been taught specific techniques with crayons or other art materials.

However, when I introduce a new technique, it's incredible to witness how it transforms the excitement and creativity in the room. So, I encourage you to consider the idea of highlighting an artist's technique from time to time when you decide to introduce an art project.

Students will find greater success when they are exposed to various methods and techniques for using different mediums and tools. You can explore artistic techniques online or at the library. I've done this myself, and I've come across some truly fantastic projects that kids can experiment with. While simply leaving crayons on the table can be enjoyable, introducing a technique empowers you to guide visual art lessons and provide the students with knowledge to expand upon.

During many of my international teacher training sessions, I've had wonderful opportunities to meet teachers from around the world and ask them questions about cultural art techniques. I've posed this question to many teachers: "Do you have family members, parents, or grandparents who engage in creative hands-on activities?"

Some teachers have responded with answers like, "Well, my grandmother knits," or another might say, "My grandfather weaves rugs." In such cases, I usually respond, "That's great! I want you to realize that your grandparents, who excel at their handicrafts, possess unique techniques.

So, you could consider bringing in some knitting samples and sharing with your students, 'Here are various ways to knit, and these are examples of my grandmother's style. She creates knitted doilies for her tables, and this is her particular technique.' You can actually demonstrate these distinctive techniques to your students."

Sometimes, as a teacher, you might have a unique

way of crafting or creating something, and you've done it so many times that you may not even realize it's a skill you excel at. Well, guess what? That's your technique. If you think about it in this way, you can say, "Oh, I have my own technique, and I can actually demonstrate to children how I do something."

Chapter Eight

ART DEVELOPS SPATIAL INTELLIGENCE

Visual Spatial Understanding

Visual arts are all about spatial understanding. Spatial learning develops from understanding the relationship between objects—the perspective of space between elements in two dimensions, geographical placement, or the position of arranged items in three-dimensional space. Spatial learning is recorded in our memory, in either the hippocampus or the medial temporal lobes of our brain.

Studying the visual arts is a significant way to improve visual spatial intelligence. Art-making teaches kids visualization. Children can conceptualize an idea straight from their imagination, then express it in either two- or three-dimensional constructing.

As children learn by making art in two and three dimensions, their long-term memories create sight patterns that are stored in the mind—spatial memories.

Sight patterns help us map relations between elements, which helps the student develop the distinguished artist's eye. Over time, this builds visual spatial intelligence.

Spatial Learning Through Dynamic and Static Experiences

Spatial art learning occurs after a child gathers tactile sensory information through two types of spatial learning, either through dynamic motion or by viewing static imagery. It's important to understand how these two experiences develop spatial learning.

Dynamic motion is physical energy that is a result of an action. When dynamic motion stays at rest, the result is static imagery to view.

It's impossible for children to truly learn visual arts

without witnessing first-hand the temporal motion of sight patterns in dynamic motion and the static imagery that results. This is how they develop spatial intelligence. It's the learning that happens cognitively through tactile sensations when a child makes art.

Static Imagery Example, page

What we have here is static information (fig. 3, in the next page). It is a static image trying to explain how two primary colors, when mixed, make a secondary color, green.

You read blue plus yellow equals green, then see blue and yellow color swatch examples, and then you can see the resulting green swatch at the bottom.

In the middle picture, blue and yellow are mixed, and the result appears to be green. You can see the girl in this picture mixing colors into green. However, this is still static imagery that you are viewing with your retinas.

It is the results of dynamic imagery at rest. It's not something you witnessed through dynamic motion. Any information you have is being pulled from your long-term memories about color mixing.

Most young children, however, do not have long-term memories to pull from cognitively. This is why we

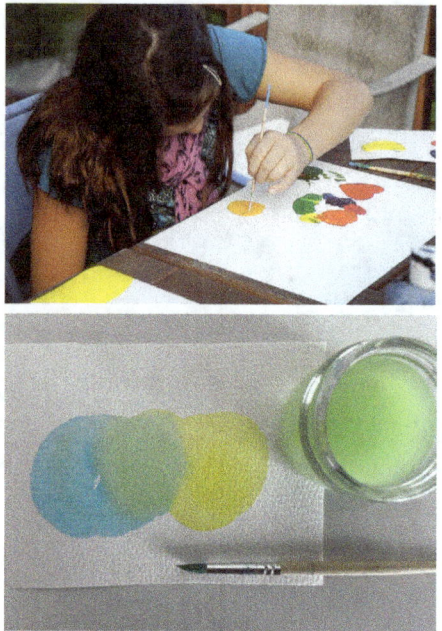

Figure 3. Mixing a secondary color, green, static information

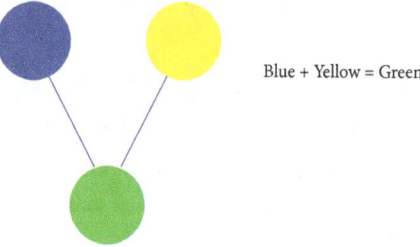

Blue + Yellow = Green

should not rely on teaching children visual arts through static imagery or verbal lectures alone.

Now, I want to show you a video to help you understand the differences between static imagery and dynamic motion learning. Go watch this video before moving forward!

Dynamic Motion Demonstration Example

View this video on YouTube:
https://www.youtube.com/watch?v=RSnM1tdA-3kM

In this video demonstration, I'm mixing primary colors into secondary colors. You will witness my dynamic motion, plus the resulting static imagery of secondary colors to view.

The purpose of this demonstration is to explain how children gain spatial intelligence by tactile dynamic motion, creating sight patterns in the memory, which is different from just viewing and learning from static imagery alone.

You can now understand my statement that it's impossible for kids to learn visual arts without experiencing temporal motion firsthand. Children must go through the process of art making to create sight patterns to store in the mind.

This becomes organized knowledge of objects in relation to oneself or a given space. Children develop color-mixing skills and predict color combinations solely by going through real-time temporal motions that are recorded in memory.

They cannot develop spatial intelligence by viewing pictures or discussing fine art imagery alone; they must record these pattern blocks of cognitive memory. If you're not allowing children to go through the artistic process firsthand, it does not qualify as visual arts literacy.

Importance of Spatial 2D and 3D Hands-On Creating

Creating art in both two and three dimensions supports good spatial awareness. Working in both dimensions develops spatial reasoning, which gives kids the ability to mentally visualize, manipulate elements, rotate objects, design form, create volume, and distinguish depth. This is how they come to understand putting together and building structures.

2D

Two-dimensional artworks have height and width. They're generally flat.

3D

Three-dimensional artworks have height, width, and depth. They take up space.

Over the course of my professional art and teaching career, I've observed the importance of creating in both dimensions. Students who had lots of opportunities to create in both dimensions have great spatial intelligence and higher success in developing conceptual ideas.

I've also met a lot of adults and artists who had no opportunity to create in either dimension, who struggle with spatial understanding and lack the skills to advance in structural design or innovative engineering careers.

It's essential that children create projects in both two and three dimensions as they grow. My longitudinal observations revealed that they should have opportunities to create in both perspectives from early childhood through adolescence. This is how they will develop spatial intelligence.

If we review the Five Domains, drawing, painting, and color theory support making two-dimensional art, and modeling and sculpture, crafting and constructing support making three-dimensional art. The Five Domains are balanced for visual spatial learning.

Now when you plan your art projects for the school year, you can identify whether you are supporting a balance of two- and three-dimensional projects. You can ask yourself, "Are my students going through dynamic motion learning?" Or, "Am I offering only static imagery information?" By understanding spatial learning, you can support a quality visual arts program.

Chapter Nine

HISTORY OF FINE ART INSTRUCTION

Where It Came from and Why We Teach this Way

Traditionally, fine art instruction includes how to draw, paint, and sculpt visual artforms. Fine art instruction can be traced back as early as circa 510 BCE and is recognized well into the twentieth century by ancient and modern great master artists. Marvelous, critically acclaimed works of art can show us examples of this continued instruction. We can see these influences in our prestigious museums worldwide.

These masterful works came about from an accumulated understanding of classical fine art principles: nature's perspective (Cole, 1976), form and shade, contour drawing, line, texture, composition, and color theory.

Fine art schools, college art courses, and public and private schools worldwide model this teaching style. As a result, this approach to teaching fine art principles is also used in art programs developed for children.

Currently, most art curricula, at the root, are designed for children with the same approach used for adults, but in a simpler manner. These programs usually start with a primer that introduces students to realism and contemporary art through the most popular classical fine artists, known as the Masters.

The Masters include Michelangelo Buonarroti, Leonardo Da Vinci, Rembrandt van Rijn, Vincent van Gogh, Pablo Picasso, Claude Monet, and others. Children are usually introduced to these artists' styles and techniques, mediums, perspectives, and famous works that influenced their particular era.

Fine art studies uncovered how the Masters evolved from creating realistic imagery to modern abstract imagery, thus paving the way for teaching visual arts. The evolution of art education and principles comes from learning how the Masters evolved and by studying their works and techniques. It's important to explain that when these famous Masters were around, it was a very different time for studying art. Equipment was scarce, and many of our current art tools were not yet invented, such as optical cameras, video recording systems, copy machines, and computers.

Artists made their living capturing images that could not be documented any other visual way. If you have ever studied art history, this is evident. Artists in previous times focused their studies on learning the illusion of painting pictures as realistically as possible. This is how memories were recorded and captured—through paintings!

Fine artists painted for profit, religious beliefs, recording historical events, or for social and political reasons. Kings and queens commissioned artists to paint their portraits to gain or maintain political power. These paintings sent messages to society, showing their symbolic tools of power and riches.

As art history explains to us and as we can see with our own eyes, the way artists expressed drawings and paintings changed over the centuries. The focus shifted away from making realistic pictures and images. At the turn of the twentieth century, artists' styles shifted to the abstract; impressionist, surrealist, avant-garde, and abstract expressionist artists emerged around this time. It became mainstream to paint and draw in these new styles. Artwork became surreal, and the human subjects were even unrecognizable at times.

Classical realism changed to more modern styles due to the development of technology and modern industrialization. Electronic devices affected this shift in art making. Electronic devices have allowed the artist to spend more time self-reflecting on creativity. Few artists are commissioned to record important memories in a realistic fashion anymore. Individual creative expression is more prevalent in modern artwork than in earlier works. Now, commissioned works give artists a chance to express visions unlike ever before.

As our great artistic styles changed, art education evolved. The Masters shaped our art culture and how we learn art today. Some of the most significant painting and drawing instructions can be traced to ideas like the cubist style.

The cubist style, or cubism, can be described as analyzing shapes. The works of Paul Cézanne (1839-1906), Georges Braque (1882-1963), and Pablo Picasso (1881-1973) show this style and technique, which is now heavily taught in fine art schools and drawing curricula today.

Other influential master artists helped shape how drawing and painting is taught. I can recall these fine art principles being introduced in my youth and adult art classes. All my art teachers spoke this language and taught in the same manner. Pick up a how-to drawing or painting book and you will recognize similar instructions.

As you can see, this is how art is presently introduced to young children as well as adults. Most likely you have been introduced to art lessons in this fashion. You may have even attempted to give art lessons to your child using this approach.

In my view, however, while studying the Masters and fine art principles is completely appropriate for adult fine art students, this method is completely wrong for children. It is not the ideal way to introduce visual arts to young students. Traditional fine art instruction interferes with a child's natural creative abilities.

Teaching children how to draw and paint too early with these old methods doesn't align with how a child develops. Teaching fine art too early can even block children artistically. In other words, our current art education method is wrong for children!

Earlier Art Experts' Theories

Discoveries and theories on child development through visual arts are scarce. At this time, there's no accurate documentation or research that shows how children develop visual art skills. Nor are there experts on this specific topic. At best, there are human behavior theorists, child psychologists, developmental psychologists, and special education specialists. In the last seventy years, these professions have helped us shape our ideas of children's creativity.

Most of these core studies are focused on children's ability to make symbolic imagery and when the developmental stages occur. The other popular and heavily researched domain is how children develop imagination and creativity.

Today, the most important contributing studies on childhood development give us insights as to how children learn to make marks, scribbles, symbolic imagery, and basic line drawings.

These are the strongest ideas we have about fine motor development, and they typically align with the stage-by-stage model, which is based on the belief in task develop as a predictable series of stages as a child matures.

These ideas originate from past psychologists like researcher Rhoda Kellogg (1979), who collected over one million drawings done by children from the US and other countries. Psychologist Jean Piaget's (1896-1980) work identifies the different logical stages of young child development. There are also current psychologists doing studies in this area, such as Howard Gardner, who has contributed his theories on multiple intelligences and studies on creativity.

However, to date, there are no experts on the topic of how children learn visual arts. There is no in-depth work on the creative child's conscious mind, how children experience visual art awareness as they grow; nor do we understand the process a child undergoes while creating art.

The creativity and the imagination of a child is not something we can study or predict. In fact, I must make a very bold statement here: The creative imagination of a human child is a hypothetical construct. In other words, it is an abstract idea used to explain theories of behaviors that relate to a cause.

Modern brain science is continuously revealing fascinating discoveries on human cognition and visual perception, which explain how our brain and eyes process information, so I am certain that old ideas about how children develop artistically will soon be challenged.

My years of working closely with children and observing people of all ages creating different types of art has shown me that this is a vast topic. The question of why one child expresses an idea better than or differently from another child is a big one. Learning about a child's creative self is no simple task, and no one observer can decode these ideas. I hope my observations will enlighten you as I share my thoughts about how children develop in the visual arts.

Chapter Ten

MODERN SCIENCE ART METHOD EMERGES

Outdated Methods Are Wrong for Children

Children do not need instruction to be truly creative. I have witnessed this with my own eyes time after time. I've seen how children can flourish into accomplished fine artists on their own!

Unfortunately, I have also worked directly with children who have lost their creative abilities after being instructed too early in their development. I've spent countless hours with such artistically frustrated children, and I've seen them struggle to make logical sense of adult visual perception too early in their development.

Modern Science Art Method Emerges

When I first started teaching visual arts, I struggled with teaching children. Although I was a talented and skilled illustrator and painter, teaching kids was challenging at first.

One of the main reasons for this struggle was the lack of information available on teaching art to children. There were no books, college courses, or online programs on how to develop art programming for youngsters. Plenty of resources focused on teaching adults and teens but not the primary grades or early childhood. Everything was geared towards how more mature students learn fine art.

My initial approach was to teach children like little artists, using the same ideas I had learned in college but with simpler lessons. However, I found it difficult to get my students to see and plan like artists. I was teaching them complex topics like the Elements and Principles of Design and asking them to look at still-life subjects to draw and paint.

Within the first few years, I learned that such tasks were too challenging for young children. It was the traditional way adult artists learned, but it wasn't suitable for them.

During those early years, I observed my son casually drawing on his own at age five after attending a guided drawing session with other children his age. He had perfectly followed directions and drawn an apple tree along with the other students.

However, when he drew on his own, he doodled and couldn't create anything realistic, even though he copied well in my classroom. His doodles were silly, abstract, and not representational like his classroom work. I found it strange that children could follow directions and copy but couldn't use those skills to create their own ideas independently.

At that stage, I realized the lessons I was teaching were not helping and were far too advanced. I started to think children needed more foundational lessons before progressing to advanced concepts. As a homeschool parent, I attracted many homeschool families to my art classes.

Unlike traditional school or after-school art programs, I had multiple age groups in my classes simultaneously. Most homeschool students attended my classes with all their siblings, ranging from toddlers to teens.

Sometimes, even the parents participated in making art. This unique setting allowed me to observe multiple ages doing exactly the same art lesson and to identify interesting patterns across the different age groups.

I noticed that younger students struggled to understand and see what I saw when I directed them to look at something, whereas older children could identify objects or images and grasp the ideas I explained.

One thing I observed was each child's visual perception. Children found it difficult to draw something they had no prior knowledge of or thoughts about. For example, a young boy struggled with my guided lessons but became excited and successful in drawing a dump truck filled with tomatoes after a weekend trip with his family.

His excitement and personal experience of seeing this empowered him to follow my directions and create an original drawing. Through these observations, I learned that three neural activities—visual perception, cognitive processing, and fine-motor capabilities—were crucial to children's ability to create art.

After recognizing this, I set aside all the ideas I learned in college and focused on nurturing these three sensory processing systems through my art lessons. My art programming developed around the phases of art development in these sensory areas for each age group.

I also discovered that too much copy-mode work stifles creativity and that children ages eight to twelve struggle with drawing realistic images due to a lack of fine-motor practice.

This often leads them to believe they are not artistic. Many foundational drawing skills are commonly overlooked before tackling complex steps in traditional art teaching models.

After years of using this teaching methodology, I became a skilled art teacher, capable of teaching almost every child at any age. While I couldn't teach toddlers to paint and draw detailed images, I could create lessons that built their foundational knowledge through process-based activities, preparing them for the next building block of art knowledge.

I could effectively teach children in the elementary grades drawing, painting, and color theory, leading to realistic imagery. By focusing on the three sensory art patterns, I could quickly assess visual art knowledge and adapt art lessons.

This became my method of teaching called the Science Art Method™ (SAM), which uses the three sensory systems to teach art, develop art lessons, and create curriculum.

SAM | Science Art Method™

This method is based on how children develop artistically through their senses and acquire fine art skills. The science art method uses the structure of the brain, working with the child's natural multisensory system and growth rate.

It supports artistic development by acknowledging hierarchical neural connections as the children process art lessons in stages. As they grow, children are wiring neural networks of information. The Science Art Method framework encompasses the three crucial parts of the child's developing sensory system:

Visual perception – the visual cortex system

Cognitive processing – the memory and neural network system

Fine motor skills – the sensorimotor movement control system

Over the last thirty years, working with students of all ages has led me to create more accessible guides for teaching visual arts to children. I firmly believe that all parents and teachers can raise creative children with the right knowledge.

I hope that Defining Visual Arts has helped you understand what art programming involves, enabling you to start planning your art program accordingly. This book is just the beginning of my series. I have many art teaching resources to guide you. Now that you understand art literacy, you can explore my Science Art Method with the book *The Way Children Make Art: The Science Art Method*. Once you have this knowledge, you can dive into my guides for early childhood or elementary art education, using some of my art curricula specifically designed for this method.

I have spent many years developing art curricula with this method in mind. These are organized into five key areas of teaching visual arts: two-dimensional painting, drawing, color theory, three-dimensional clay modeling, and crafting. These areas form the foundation for developing the three key neurological components using the SAM method.

Defining Visual Arts

Chapter Eleven

Moving Forward With Art Literacy

Through the chapters of this book, we've explored the essentials of teaching visual arts to children. Together, we've uncovered why visual art education serves as a fundamental pillar for early childhood and elementary grades worldwide. We've examined how visual art standards provide a guiding framework for educators. Now, it's time to take that knowledge and put it into practice.

How can you bring art literacy into your organization, classroom, or home? How can you integrate these concepts into your lessons or programs in a meaningful way? While there's no single "right" way to get started, I want to outline a potential framework to help you begin.

Four Stages to Get Started

Below are four stages that can guide you in applying art literacy principles to your teaching and program planning. Whether you're an individual teacher or part of a larger institution, these steps offer a simple roadmap.

Stage 1: Share the Art Literacy Foundations

Begin by introducing the principles of art literacy to your team, administrators, or fellow educators. Consider hosting a meeting or informal gathering where you can share what you've learned from this book. You could even create a book club to deepen your engagement with the material. Discuss the importance of teaching visual art standards and explain how it fosters creativity, critical thinking, and cultural understanding in children. To help with this, provide handouts and key resources found at the back of this book. Use these sessions to share successes, brainstorm solutions to challenges, and expand your resource pool. Reflect on the outcomes of your initial art literacy projects and make adjustments as needed.

Example Activity

Create a one-page visual aid listing the key art elements (line, color, shape, texture, etc.) alongside examples of how they can be woven into real-life lessons. Share it with colleagues and discuss how these elements apply across subjects (for instance, symmetry in mathematics or color theory in science). You can download a free list of the art elements to share here.

Stage 2: Connect Art Elements to Lessons

Take the foundational knowledge of art standards and directly tie it to your art lessons or storybooks about art. Start small by incorporating one art element at a time into your classroom art activities. For example, introduce "line" in art history by exploring how line art was used in ancient cave paintings.

If you need guidance on lesson design using art elements, check out my art guides for both elementary and early childhood education. These guides include great examples how it is done. You can order them by following the links in the back of this book. By connecting art elements to other lessons, you make art literacy a natural and integrated part of the broader curriculum.

Stage 3: Plan Art Lessons

Start developing a curated list of art projects that intentionally connect to art literacy. For example, you might map out a quarter or semester focusing on specific themes, such as "Art Across Cultures" or "Nature and Art." Within each theme, plan age-appropriate projects that incorporate multiple art elements and guide children through the four stages of the artistic process. Above all start simple, and experiment with a few art lessons to get the hang of how to identify art literacy in your activities.

Stage 4: Invest in Professional Development

To truly advance your integration of art literacy, consider enrolling in my online workshops or courses focused on visual art education. Working with experts can provide you with new techniques, fresh ideas, and additional frameworks to enrich your teaching practice If your school or organization has the budget, invite a guest speaker or trainer with experience in art literacy. I'm here to partner with you on this journey.

Moving Forward With Confidence

From the concepts in this book, you now have the tools to build a standards-aligned art literacy program for children. Educators and programs that have implemented these strategies have seen tremendous success in improving not only artistic skills but also creativity and critical thinking in students. This is achievable for you with the knowledge you now hold.

Lastly

Finally, if you loved this book (or found it helpful), please consider leaving a review on Amazon or the retailer where you purchased it. Your feedback not only supports my work but also helps others discover the principles that could transform their teaching practices.

Thank you for purchasing this book. Together, we're shaping a world where art literacy thrives in every corner, bringing joy, connection, and creative possibility to children everywhere.

I wish you the best on this journey.
Keep creating!

Spramani Elaun

Defining Visual Arts

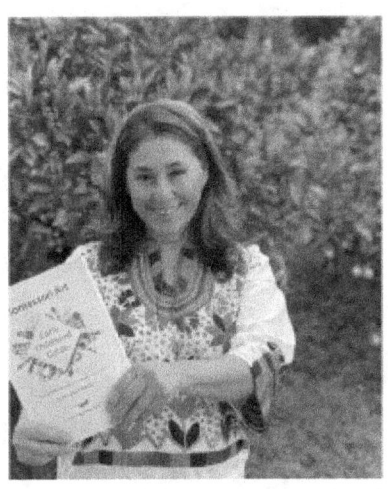

About the Author

Spramani Elaun is the author of several art education books. She is a homeschooling mom, an art teacher with a natural teaching method, and the founder of Nature of Art ® art school and art supply company. She lives in San Diego with her family.

After spending thousands of hours teaching young children art, she now supports teachers and parents on how to use her time-tested visual art methods.

Spramani teaches art classes, trains teachers, hosts art workshops at education conferences, guest speaks, and hosts art events internationally.

Her educational background includes degrees and certification in visual communication, graphic design, fine arts, painting, multimedia, offset printing, digital, and business marketing management.

Resources

Author's Contact

Spramani Elaun
Nature of Art®
P.O. Box 443 Solana Beach,
CA 92075
U.S. 1 + (760) 652-5194

http://montessori-art.com/
http://www.ecokidsart.com/

Email: Info@Spramani.com
WhatsApp: +1 (760) 652-5194
WeChat ID: Spramani-Art Teacher

Instragram
https://www.instagram.com/nature.of.art.for.kids/
Linkedin
https://www.linkedin.com/in/ecokidsart/

Defining Visual Arts

Author Services:

- Keynote Speaker
- Live Workshops
- Venue Sponsorship
- Corporate Creative Events
- Teacher Art Training – Online, In-Service
- Educational/Seminar
- Video Art Training – Online
- Premium Art Supply Materials
- Art Teaching Blueprint™ – Online Certification

Resources

Books

Nurturing Children in the Visual Arts Naturally
ISBN-13: 978-0991626403
Clay Play ISBN-13: 978-0991626441
Kids Painting ISBN-13: 978-0991626410
Kids Color Theory ISBN-13: 978-0991626434
The Way Children Make Art ISBN-979-8991256117
Introducing Visual Arts to the Montessori Classroom
ISBN-13: 978-0991626427
Early Childhood Art Guide ISBN 9780991626496
Montessori Early Childhood Art Guide
ISBN 9780991-626472
Montessori Art: The Essential Elementary Guide - Second Plane
6-12, ISBN 9798991256100

Defining Visual Arts

Order Curriculums

Painting Curriculum, 57 brushstroke Lessons
Painting Work – Art Album (Montessori Elementary)
Kids Color Theory Curriculum, 37 mixing Lessons
Clay Modeling, 27 Lessons
KidsDrawing Curriculum 41 Lessons (Elementary)
Kids Drawing Curriculum 14 Lessons (Early Childhood)

Kids Crafting & Constructing Curriculum

Order Curriculum Here, Montessori-Art.com

Resources

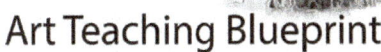

Art Teaching Blueprint

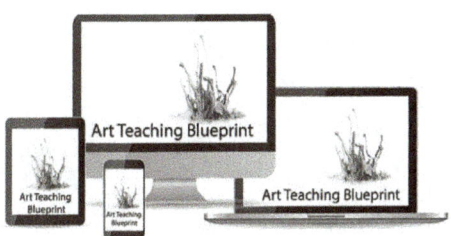

Get Art Certifed

Online Digital Course

Art Teaching Blueprint is comprehensive and broad in scope; it lays the foundation for understanding how children learn art so that you can start implementing art lessons into your classroom. Certification or self-pace is offered.

Learn more by visiting Montessori-Art.com

Resources

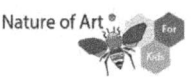 Nature of Art

Free Resources, follow QR codes for book enhancements

Join Spramani's Weekly Art Newsletter

Elementary Art Materials List

Phases of Art Video Training

Elements of Art List (Artsy Terms) List

Resources

Curriculums

Paint Curriculum, 57 brushstroke Lessons ISBN 978-0991626465

Painting Work – Art Album (Elementary)

Kids' Color Theory Curriculum, 37 mixing Lessons

Clay Modeling, 27 Lessons

Kids' Drawing Curriculum 41 Lessons (Elementary)

Kids' Drawing Curriculum 14 Lessons (Early Childhood)

Kids' Crafting Curriculum

Order Curriculum Here

Resources

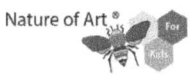

Shop Nature of Art®
Premium Children's Art Supplies

Store.EcoKidsArt.com

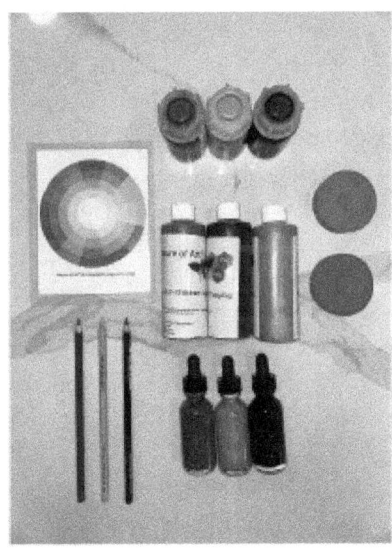

The Way Children Make Art

If you are developing an art curriculum or teaching art to children—from toddlers to teens—The Way Children Make Art is an invaluable resource. This book offers essential insights into how children learn to create art. (Hint: very differently than adults!)

What can you learn from this book?

How and when children develop fine motor function
An art education method based on science
What an age-appropriate arts program looks like
How children learn to create
...and more!

Over the past three decades as an art educator, Spramani Elaun has developed her trademarked Science Art Method (SAM), based upon her own experience and the most current neuroscience. Here she delves into childhood development of fine motor function, cognitive abilities, visual and tactile processing, and spatial intelligence.

As you come to understand your students' phases of neurological growth, you can design age-appropriate art lessons that will nurture their development and encourage their creativity.

The Way Children Make Art

The Science Art Method™

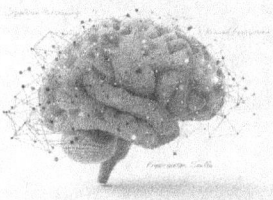

Spramani Elaun

Notes

Notes

Notes